Henry H Miller

Phillips Memorial

Henry H Miller

Phillips Memorial

ISBN/EAN: 9783337386474

Printed in Europe, USA, Canada, Australia, Japan

Cover: Foto ©ninafisch / pixelio.de

More available books at **www.hansebooks.com**

1300
PHILLIPS OF CROSBY

1776

PHILLIPS

US

PHILLIPSBURGH

BY

HENRY H. MILLER

CHICAGO
1897

PHILLIPS
MEMORIAL

BY
HENRY H. MILLER.

PHILLIPS GENEALOGIES

REV. GEORGE PHILLIPS, son of Christopher PHILLIPS was born at Rainham St. Martin, near Raynham, in ... of Crailion, County Norfolk, Eng, in ... 1593. He graduated at Cains College Cambridge as B.A. 1613, - ... his orders he took ... He married the daughter of Rev. Sergan ... a native ... a minister at Boxacre Suffolk Co. and suffering from the persecution ... that ... on the Non-Conformists he determined to ... New England and cast his lot with the Puritans. He sailed for America on the ship ARBELLA - said to be the first vessel crossing ... the Puritans ... April 12th 1630. He was fellow passenger with the Gov. John Winthrop and Sir Richard Saltonstall ... one of the Chaplains during the voyage. In "Sprague's memoirs ... is ... a quote ... from Gov. Winthrop's journal "It ... perhaps ... gave ... counsel to all the company ... in his ... and they have much to bless god for him." He landed at Salem, June 12th and his wife died soon after, from hardships ... during the voyage. ... Winthrop some years later some of the "She took her New England on her way to heaven" Rev. Phillips was chosen the first minister of the Church of Watertown Mass. - ... by Sir Fred Dobsonals as he says in his journal "a part of his plantation" ... a meeting house, ... to some numerous ... friends, in an almost ... Others

Rodger Clap who came from England on the Arabella in 1630, and who has left some writings says of Mr. Phillips, when telling of the times just after landing "The meeting place was under a tree, where I have heard Mr. Phillips preach many a good sermon."

He died July 1st 1644, and an entry on Gov. Winthrop's journal of this year is as follows "July 2nd George Phillips was buried to day. He was the first pastor of the church at Watertown, — a godly man and specially gifted." "Family Memorials" by Prof. Edward E. Salisbury of New Haven, in which is given Phillips Genealogy, gives an account of Rev. George Phillips by Cotton Mather. Among the first paragraphs is this (written at the time of his death 1644) "There was one George who was indeed among the first Saints of New England, and that Excellent man of our land was Mr. George Phillips." The account concludes with the following "He laboured under many bodily infirmities but was especially viable to the Cholick, the extremity of one fit whereof was the wind which carried him along it, into the Haven of Eternal rest, on the first day of July 1644, much desired and lamented by his Church in Watertown." A "writer in Harpers" says "A Phillips crossed the water with John Winthrop, and from him are descended a long line of Ministers, Judges, Councilors, Legislators, and Governors, — a sterling race, tempered just and high minded." . . . . . "In Boston Hall — the Library of the Theological School, in the grand halls of the Academies of Andover and Exeter, and in the Memorial Hall at Harvard College, one may see hanging on the walls, portraits, of one and another man and woman of this family, which belong to the untitled nobility of New England, representing the best element of life here — not that which always carries bodily to flow of politically, but that which . . . .

Rev. George Phillips wife died at Watertown June 27, 1681. The children are

Samuel	Born England 1625 1st wife			Theophilus	Born Watertown May 28, 1636
Elizabeth	"	"	"	Annabel	"	" Dec. 1637
Zerobabel	"	Watertown Apr 6 1632		Ephraim	"	June 1640
Jonathan	"	"	Nov 10 1633	Obadiah	"	died young
				Abigail		

The founders of Phillips Academy, descendants of Rev. Geo. Phillips, cut the Phillips coat of arms, in stone, over the entrance of the main hall, and used them on their publications, stationery &c. In later years Hon. Wendell Phillips, another descendant, made very careful investigation in England into the English Phillips genealogy, and claimed that the Phillips arms in use at Andover by the Phillips Academy, were not the proper arms of the family, but that Christopher Phillips was undoubtedly descended from "Phillips of Crostwick" and he says "I have traced the ancestry of our family — without a break, back to about 1200." Below are the arms of "Phillips of Crostwick"

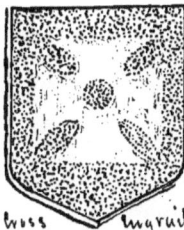

According to English authorities on heraldry, these arms — without a crest, are "Squires arms". Also the Maltese cross is not used in the arms of any family who do not trace back to the Crusades "or, a Maltese cross engrailed pierced in the centre or."

(or — Gothic with gold. gu. — red)

REV. SAMUEL PHILLIPS (son of George) was born in England 1625 — probably at Boxford Suffolk. He married Sarah Appleton born at Reydon Eng. 1629 daughter of Samuel Appleton. He graduated at Harvard College 1650 in one of the first classes after this college was founded — was settled as minister of Rowley Mass. He had eleven children. George, the eighth was

He lived at _____, _____ April ___ 1696 _____, _____ "His wife" died July __, 1711. Thomas Gage in History of Rowsy _____ "one of him". He was highly esteemed for his piety, and _____ _____ _____ of _____ order." A _____ monument was erected to him and his wife by Jonathan Phillips of Boston on which is inscribed a long list of their distinguished descendants.

REV. GEORGE PHILLIPS (son of Samuel) Born June 3rd 1664, at Rowley — graduated at Harvard Coll. 1686, was settled as a minister, first in Mass. — went to Long Island and was settled at Setauket in the town of Brookhaven in 1697. was not ordained there until 1702, when he was given land by the town. His _____ afterwards gave him two hundred acres more, on condition that he would remain as their pastor all his life, which he did. He is most highly spoken of in Thompson's History of L. Island, and in "Sprague's Annals of the American pulpit." one writer says "A man of solid Value with a happy flow of wit that _____ that rendered his company and conversation always agreeable." Another — probably of a more serious turn says "A good man, not indulged in wit and drollery" The fact that his church wished to keep him as their pastor for life, seems to indicate that his "wit and drollery" pleased the most of his hearers. Thompsons History of L. I. says "Few families have been more distinguished for liberal donations to religious and literary institutions than the Phillips." Rev. George Phillips married Sarah Hallett born March 19. 1673. daughter of William and Sarah Hallett Newtown L. I. They had six children. George, the first child was born April 1st 1698. _____ Phillips _____ _____ and was buried in the Presbyterian burying ground. About 1830, a _____ _____ _____ was erected by Phillips Lord to _____.

GEORGE PHILLIPS. (son of Rev. George). was born at Brookhaven L.I.
April 1, 1698. He lived at Smithtown L.I.—married Elizabeth daughter of Timothy
and Sarah Mills. born Aug. 16, 1705. Her parents were of Jamaica and Smithtown. They had seven children as follows—

Samuel. Born 1728.   James Born 1736.   Moses Born. March 8, 1747.
Sarah   " 1730.   Elizabeth " 1737.
George   " 1734.   Mary   " 1741.

From the "Col. Phillips family bible" N.Y. Historical Mss. and many other sources,

MOSES PHILLIPS. (son of George) was born at ~~Brookhaven~~ Smithtown L.I.
March 8, 1747. He went to Orange Co. N.Y. about 1765. He married Sarah daughter
of Henry Wisner of Goshen. Jan. 22, 1768 ("Record early N.Y. marriages).
He settled and founded Phillipsburgh on the Wallkill. on land that was
his wifes dower. Built a dam and mills on each side of the stream—one
a grist. the other a woolen Mill. which latter he carried on until near
the time of his death. He was Commissioned a Major in the 5th Ulster
Co. Regt. in service during the Revolutionary War. "Calendar of N. York
Historical Mss." (Albany N.Y. 1868. from Mss. in office Secty. of State) Vol. I. P. 177
gives the following. "Field and Staff Officers 5th Ulster Co Regt."

        Col. James Clinton   Commission dated 1775
        Lt. Col. James McClaughry   "   "
        Maj. Isaac Kennedy   "   "
        Major. Moses Phillips   "   "
        Adjutant. George Denniston   "   "
        Qr. Master. Alexander Trimble   "   "

Same Authority Vol I. P. 779. gives the record of proceedings of the N.Y. Prov-
incl Congress—resolutions passed relating to 5th Ulster Co. Regt. [...] [illegible]

Henry Wisner ... the proper persons to ... a ... ... that the ... at Philadelphia. (Revolutionary History, ... 1857, State ... ... Revolutionary ... ... His original commission is in possession of Fred Phillips of ... ... and a photographic copy ... ... From the ... of this ... (1775) he ... ... to be ... as Major and in the ... Regiments. ... ... and Haldimane ... ... give the following Distribution of Haldimane's ... ... Wisner's Regt. ... ... on active service from Aug 5th to Sept 3rd 1779, under command of Major Moses Phillips.

HENRY WISNER, the father of the wife of Moses Phillips, and so ... ... of the inhabitants of this, was a man of much distinction in the history of New York, and this American Colonies both before and during the Revolution. His ... service was continuous from 1764 to 1795. His Grand father was one of the first settlers of Goshen 1714. He was Johannes Wisner, a Swiss — an officer in the Swiss contingent of the army of the Prince of Orange — and came to America 1713, after the conclusion of peace by the "Treaty of Utrecht" in Queen Annes reign, and came to Goshen with the first ... settlers. ★

★ ... History of Orange C. N.Y. and other authorities say that the "Wawayanda patent" which ... all this part of Orange Co. and was dated 1703, was first settled on the banks of Goshen ... ... in the county ... on ... ... Denn ... ... his original patentee, ... got his ... in long island and New York in 1712 and 1713. He ... this an old ... dated 1704, a will ... by ... Edw. ... Phillips the ... Who made ... Moses Phillips to ... D ... ... of the ... ... of Christopher Denn ... of the ... ...

Mr. Wisner served as a member of the New York Provincial Assembly from 17.. to 17.., a member of the first Committee to insist... on the grounds of differing between the colonies and the American... — a member of the First Continental Congress, convened at Philadelphia in the fall of 1774, and signed the celebrated "Non-importation Agreement" — was elected at the annual town meeting of Goshen, April ..th 1775 (so and so... Vol. 1, P. ..) as a delegate to the Provincial Congress of New York. By and by that body was chosen one of the N.Y. delegates to the Second Continental Congress. When he took part in the various political measures regarding the Choice of a Commander in Chief for the American armies. His name was not affixed on the copy of the Declaration of Independence which was signed by those present July 4th 1776. Nor is his biography given in "Biographies of Signers of the Declaration of Independence" which was published long in the making, and which the years set down show alone who have I now was proven to be Signers. There is no doubt however but that Henry Wisner did sign afterwards — probably in ... as the Congressional records show he had returned from New York and was in his seat. (Some members did not sign until October). There are they many who he could have signed this instrument. The Congressional records show a resolution passed July 19th that all the members of this Congress who are now absent New York Signers have the to the Capitol that signed. There is plenty of ... or ... from the "Evidence Appendix of the Declaration "Appendix to Epitome of American Biography... Vol. 6, P..." under the head of "Henry Wisner — He has been indicted ...... "...". He voted for the Declaration of Independence and was the only one of the N.Y. delegates that did. He was one of the most radical of all the Whigs, and of none of British oppression; of that ..., and had voice for years ... he was ....

8

The account in the Cyclopedia goes on. "Before the instrument was engrossed on parchment and ready for signature, he went to New York to attend the Provincial Congress, of which he was a member." This is also shown by the records of Congress. His feelings towards the British expressed before hostilities commenced is shown by an incident related in "Eager's History of Orange Co. N.Y." Page 450, where he is speaking of the building of a new court house at Goshen. To replace a similar one built of wood in 1737, a new one of stone and two stories high was built in 1773 (two years before Lexington). A question arose as to where the Kings Arms should be placed, one wanted them hung in one place on the walls, and another proposed another location. "Henry Wisner stood a patriot" stood by and silently heard the discussion, at last he spoke "Give me the arms and I will place them where no one will object" he seizes the emblem and dashing it against the side of the building, broke a blow from a hammer broke it into fragments "Such contempt of the emblem of royalty, in open day, at these early period, was certainly evidence of the intense feeling which foreshadowed the results of the Revolution." It is recorded of him, that while serving in the New York assembly in 1777 (he was elected Senator for the Middle District in 1777 and served until 1782) he stated before that body, that he owed 3000 pounds to two men, that he had paid one of them and wished to pay the other but that as the man was serving in the Kings army, he could not do so. The members of the assembly voted that he should pay the amount into the hands of the Treasurer of the State, in the presence of witnesses, taking a receipt for same and that should cancel the debt. The "National Cyclopedia of American Biography" Vol 5 P 464 under the head of "Henry Wisner patriot" in concluding "Wisner's way of placing the

... the Hudson. Mounted cannon and manning ... of his own expense. Seriously annoyed the British in their navigation of the river. ... a commission consisting of Prof. ... Henry Wisner and ... to ... the Highlands of the Hudson and report ... and plans for building fortifications. The result was the building at West Point of Fort ... and its out works including Fort Putnam ... In this work there are references to the public service of this man in following places.

Vol I Pages ... — 189 — ... — ... — ...

" II " 97 — 98 — 99 — 109.

In "Colonial history of New York" he is mentioned in following places.
Vols. 15 Pages ... — 125 — 145 — 133 — ...

There is ... "record" and it is all very good. He died March ... 1790. aged 70. and was buried in the "Phillips burying ground" at Phillips ... there are many Phillips buried here — John Frank Smith town J.C. — Descendants of ... Moses Phillips brothers and sisters who ... New Island. The Revolutionary records of New York show that Smith town furnished to the Continental army Phillips ... New London Hist. N.Y. Doc. 16.—

---

* In "Memorial of Henry Wisner by Franklin Burdge C. is stated that the burial place of Henry Wisner is unknown. This is true as his grave was found at Phillisburg by Miss Sarah S. Phillips and Robt. Robb ... descendants. The ... of births is not given ... The ... by ... the will ...

The children of _____ Moses Phillips are as follows —

	Born		Died	
GABRIEL NEWTON	Born ___ ___ 1769.	Died ___ 7. 1849.
GEORGE	December 1770.	"	April 13. 1849
HENRY WISHER	" May 15. 1773.	"	May 30. 1813.
MOSES	" ___ ___ 1776.	"	___ ___ 1849.
WILLIAM	" " 9. 1778.	"	Sept 1. 1800.
LEWIS	" " 20. 1783.	"	___. 1861.
SARAH	" May 19. 1750.	"	Sept 2. 1781.
SAMUEL	" July 11. 1755.	"	Oct 20. 1798.
ELIZABETH	" Oct 27. 1757.	"	" 23. 1856.

He died at Phillips ____ Sept 9. 1815. His wife died ____ Oct 10. 1810. They were buried in the Phillips burying ground.

___

COL WILLIAM PHILLIPS (son of Moses) Born Jany 9. 1778 at Phillips ____ N.Y. He married ____ ____ June 8. 1804. She was born Jany 3. 1788. and was of a family of ____ ____ in the history of New York. They were ____ from ____ ____ ____ the great Dutch ____ ____ in 1673. ____ great ____ ____ English ____ ships in ____ ____ ____ his ____ to New Amsterdam, now New York, ____ ____ in possession ____ the English since 1665. ____ ____ his ____ into New York ____ ____ possession of the ____ of ____ a Dutch Governor. ____ the ____ of the ____ to ____ ____ out ____ in their ____ ____ ____ ____ was called "Kill the D__l" he ____ ____ ____ The colony soon after settled down no ____ ____ he as his ____ the "____ in ____" he ____ ____ ____

He returned to put in boards, and soon he had made cloth. The business grew and was very prosperous til the time transfer was made for the Convenience for the trade, and bought before a portion of the province of this trade but it is believed in New York. The trade was sent down the river &c and the trade toward then the river was frozen this delivery of cloth was more expensive and simple. The Colonel would sometimes go with one of these large loads of cloth, and as he did not like the noise of things that was a long term in the streets, only for use on his horses, from the bonds of his city was reduced and when no ordinary required him ...

... appearance was that intelligence of the master ... the master's interest had come to this part of the country to see the new town in his new carriage, to this first ordinary place, he made his ... extended contribution for the ... he ... as ... Duchastine, ministers of all denominations ... be heard ... of this house, and to ... Duchastine ... Chambers of ... having both time attractive ... for the kindness, generosity and characters of Col. Phillips were very ... noted, he ... wages slaves ... he were free and paid their wages, ... was also the best of ... comissation with his firm in New York State, there it is at this time quite a settlement of colored people near Phillips works and lands ... the liberated slaves of Col. Phillips, and the father Major Moore. In the very hard times following the crash of 1837, a great part of his very large wealth was tied through Endorsements to aid his friends. He proved himself above the character of common report, his life was ...

3 SAMUEL. " Oct. 6. 18__ " ___ ___ " June 6. 18__

4 JULIA. " Aug. __. 1811 " May __. 1858 " Feby. 7. 18__

5 HENRY LEWIS. April 13. 1813 " Jan __. 1848. " May 15. 1810.

6 SARAH EVERTSON. " " 11. 1815. ___ ___ " April 26. 1810.

7 ELIZABETH PAYNE. " March 30. 1817. Decem. 12. 1807. " March 11. 1843.

8 WILLIAM NITCHE. " June 1. 18__ " Oct. 7. 1850. " Feby 4. 1845.

9 THOMAS SCOTT. " Sept. 15. 1853 " Jany. 30. 1857. " April 21. 1810.

10 NICHOLAS EVERTSON. " Jany. 10. 1850 " Sept. 6. 1870. " Jany 13. 1845

11 EDGAR (L.) " April 5. 1857 " May 6. 1857

---

1 JOHN EVERTSON Born March __. 1805 at Phillipsburgh N.Y. He graduated at Williams College 1875 — Studied law and practiced at Goshen N.Y. He married Elizabeth Cuthman. daughter of Henry G. Wisner of Goshen. He died Oct. 17. 18__. His children are as follows —
SARAH WISNER. Born Sept. 21. 1835. Died April 19. 1840.
ANNA EVERTSON. " April 1. 1838. Married John H. Conner April 13. 1875 She now resides in New York City.
HARRIET HORNBECK. Born July 6. 1840. She now resides at the old family home at Goshen. Mrs John E. Phillips died at Goshen
18

---

1 SAMUEL B. Born Sept. 18. 1806. at Phillipsburgh N.Y. Died October 26. 1807.

SAMUEL, Born ... at ... Died June ... 1...

JULIA, ... 1810, ...

...

SARAH EVERTSON, (...) born ... 1841.

HENRY HORNBECK, " " " ... 1843.

WILLIAM YOUNG " " ... 9, 1848.

JULIA PHILLIPS " " ... 7, 1853.

SARAH EVERTSON (...) Born at Ridgebury Orange Co. N.Y. (...Phillips...) March 2, 1841. She was educated at the Brooks Collegiate Institute at Troy N.Y. and now resides in New York City.

HENRY HORNBECK, (...) Born March 9, 1843, at ... N.Y. ...

...recovered of a severe sickness, ?... from his ?. After ?
in ? 1861, he went to Chicago, where he was employed as clerk and
bookkeeper in the office of Phillips ?? his cousin. He became a member
of a military company — the Ellsworth Zouaves — when the "firing
on Sumpter" caused it to offer its services. This was Colonel
E. E. Williams, the first volunteer troops that left Chicago for the war.
He was made Drum major to teach the new "Zouave facings" it was
expected to go with them to ? Illinois, which was then "the front." Jos. ?
? troops. His father however, as a ? "? is going to the
war" ? "Uncle Joe" (Phillips) came to the city from his home in
? Illinois, was ?... to this, on account of ? age. He said,
"?, the boys must stand back and ? in the war at home." He was
? on its "? ?" — everything was made satisfactory with
?, ? — a "man" — as ? ? of ? from another ?
Commission officer, was given "? ?" to serve his country in the
Battery & ? remained in Chicago as ? ? of the Second Battery
B, not yet ready to go forward. In the summer of the next year — 1862,
however, when the call for "Three hundred thousand more" came, ?
with the free consent of his father, took his "chance," in a company of
his ? and ? mates — Co. N ?... ? ? ? ? ...

* Ellsworth Zouaves were then famous as "the finest drilled body of men in the country"
"a company of trained athletes" as ... the newspapers had it. "Ellsworth men" were
in demand to drill the new recruits in ?. The most tragic death of Col. Ellsworth
in May 61, caused intense ?... through the country and particularly in Chicago
where he first had commanded the company that made him famous.
This "Institute" was killed in one of the first engagements of the ?, ? ...

He served continuously from Aug 2, 1862 to Nov. 20, 1866 — was promoted
— 1st Lieut. 31st U.S. Infty. (Resign) 1864. — 1st Lieut. (Regular) June 1864. — Captain
Oct. 1864. — brevited for good service to Major March 13, 1865 — Served as
such until Oct. 1866, when he received a Commission as Lieutenant in
39th Infty. U.S.A. (regular army) He did not muster on this however
not wishing to remain in the army in time of peace, but mustered out
with his regiment in November at New Orleans La. He came north
over to Peoria Ills. where Aug. 14, 1871 he married _Diadamia_, the
daughter of _Sidney Pulsifer_ of Peoria Ills. following are their children

<u>LOUIS PULSIFER</u> Born Aug 5, 1872.

<u>HENRY PHILLIPS</u> " Feby 12, 1874.

<u>WILLIAM YOUNG</u> (Hansel) Born Oct 9, 1845. at Ridgebury N.Y.
He married <u>Mary</u> daughter of <u>J.W. Hansel</u> of Peoria Ills. 1872
Their children are as follows.

<u>AGNES HANSEL</u> Born April 25, 1873.

<u>MARY ELIZABETH</u> " Novmr 17, 1875. Died Sept 11, 1877

<u>AGNES HANSEL</u> (Miller) Born April 25, 1873. at Peoria Ills. She married
<u>Jesse P. Gensler</u> of Eldorado Kans. Sept 12, 1894. They have one daughter
<u>JESSIE CORWIN</u> (Gensler) Born July 8, 1896. This is the only one
(in this line) in the 11th Generation from <u>Christopher Phillips</u> (born 1636)

6 HENRY LEWIS (Son of Col. William) Born April 13. 1815. at Phillipsburgh. He married Mary Thompson Jany 4. 1844. He succeeded
his father in the management of the farm at Phillipsburgh.
In 1850 he removed to a farm near Honesdale Pa. on which he
lived until his death May 15. 1886. His wife died at Goshen N.Y.
There were no children.

---

7. ELIZABETH PAYNE Born March 30, 1817. at Phillipsburgh.
She was educated at
        She married Dr Henry Hendrick of St Andrews Orange
Co. N.Y. December 10. 1857. They resided at St. Andrews and Phillipsburgh
She died March 11. 1863. There was one child as follows,
WILLIAM PHILLIPS (Hendrick) Born   1859 Died Aug. 18. 1860.

---

8 SARAH EVERTSON. Born April 11. 1815 at Phillipsburgh. Died
April 26 1816.

---

8 WILLIAM RITCHIE. June 1. 1830. at Phillipsburgh N.Y.
He and his brother Thomas went to Illinois in 1849. - Engaged
in the Grain and Commission business at Copperas Creek Landing on the Illinois river in 1850. They moved to Galesburg Ills
in 1855. where they erected the first grain elevator there built
They continued in the Grain and Commission business. -
William residing in Galesburg and his brother Thomas in
Chicago - under the firm name of Phillips Bros. and
later Phillips & Carr & Ward. another partner being admitted.

In 1882 the firm was dissolved, all the partners retired from active business, and each with a large fortune. He was very large and at one time the firm of Phill (grain firms) was one of the largest in the West.

William married Ann McKinnie, daughter of Ewing of Knoxville Ills. Oct. 2. 1850. He died Feb. at Galesburg and was buried at Knoxville Ills. bes. sister Julia (Miller) He was for many years one of that village – a man of much prominence in his and very much respected. His children are as fo

1 JANE EWING .   Born July 5. 1857.

2 WILLIAM EVERTSON   "   June 22. 1862.

3 MARGARET CAMPBELL.   "   March 28, 1866.

4 FREDRICK WISNER   "   June. 13, 1871.

---

1 JANE EWING. Born. July 5. 1857. at Galesburg Ills. Henry W. Chase son of Dr. Chase of Galesburg. Here they now reside at that place. The following are their

PHILLIPS MAURICE (Chase) Born April 6. 1886.

MARGARET EVERTSON . "   December 22. 1889.

---

2 WILLIAM EVERTSON. Born June 22. 1862 at Galesb He married Carrie daughter of ____ Atkins of Iowa 10th 1888. Their children are as follows.

WILLIAM RITCHIE JR. Born Aug. 5. 1889 Died Feb. 9. 18

FREDRICK WISNER Born. Jan. [?] [?].

3. MARGARET CAMPBELL. Born. March [?] [?] at Galesburg Ills. She
married [?] P. Hoover. son of Joseph Hoover of Galesburg Ills. The following
are their children.
ANNA EWING (Hoover) Born. November 21. 1880.
EDWIN K.   "   Died. 13. 1892

4. FREDRICK WISNER. Born. June 13. 187[?] at Galesburg Ills. He mar-
ried Cora. daughter of [?] [?] of Galesburg Oct. 10. 1893.
Their children are as follows ~
WILLIAM MARSH Born. July 23. 1895.

THOMAS SCOTT. Born. Sept. 14. 1843 at Philipsburgh N.Y. He [?]
[?] [?] his brother William went to Illinois ~ lived to Princton Bureau
Co. where [?] [?] [?] living ~ was [?] of Rev. Abraham Wilson
The brothers went into the [?] grain and commission business ~ first at
[?] [?] [?] [?] on the Illinois river and afterwards at Galesburg
and Chicago. The firm was Phillips & Bro. [?] [?] years [?] [?]
[?] grain business. [?] [?] [?] George Carmichael. was
admitted and the firm [?] changed to Phillips & Carmichael.
Thomas resided in Chicago from 1886. until the time of his death. April
21. 1890. He married Martha [?]. the daughter of Dr. David [?] [?]
          June 20. 1867. Their children are as follows.
HARRIET CLALE Born. March 17. 1863.

0 <u>NICHOLAS EVERTSON</u>

exhibition." Wm Bross selected for Nicholas to learn and "speak" some speech by Thomas Jefferson, or Andrew Jackson, for in those days his politics were as radically Democratic as in later years they were Whig only Republican. All of Nicholas' undercurrents were strong Whig but found no fault, and learned and recited his speech to Mr Bross' entire satisfaction. He also learned and recited to his brother-in-law - Mr Miller "Webster's reply to Hayne of South Carolina". On the evening of the exhibition, many of the audience knew that "Dick" Phillips was to "speak" and they also knew that _____ was a _____ and would not tolerate anything Whig in his reading. When his turn came Dick took the platform and gave them _____ in spite of all the _____ attempts of Mr Bross to _____ off the programme. The _____ _____ said _____ Gov Bross _____ _____ Dick Phillips _____ _____ _____.

Soon _____ Nicholas and his _____ Nicholas _____ _____ to _____ Fulton Co, Ills, where lived _____ - Rev Herman Wilson, the _____ of _____ _____ _____ _____ _____ Nicholas, was living. Rev Wilson was the _____ _____ a colony of "Jersey Dutchmen" that made a settlement in Fulton ab 1837. He was their pastor, _____ and _____ _____ as well known and greatly respected in this part of Illinois as "Dominie Wilson" He died at a great age in 1860, leaving many descendants living in and about the town that he had founded and named. Young Nicholas was employed in a store belonging to his uncle until 1854, when he and his brother _____ _____ _____ _____

... and ... her "Virginia Poe" ... ...
... ... the ... and ... ... prove his
... of his country. He is ... ... no the "best
children." ...

...

...

...

by his ... William ... H ... in ... they ... ...

... ...

...

...

...

...

... Eliza Ives.
September, 18?0, ... had one child
... ... James.

__HENRY IVES.__ ...

__LEWIS EGERTSON__ ... Died Sept. 23, 1856

__WILLIAM WENDELL__ ... ...

EDGAR I. ... born April ?, 1847 at Phillipsburg N.Y.
He entered Williams College ... ... of the class of 1867.
His ... ... strong before his time ... ...
... He went to his home in Phillipsburg and did not
return to complete his course. He went to Cleveland O. in
September 1867 and remained there until April 1868 ...

went to Fairview Fulton Co. Ills. where he studied Medicine with
Dr. Gaddis whose wife was his cousin — the daughter of Rev. Abraham
Wilson. In 1852 he and his brother Nicholas went to California
— crossing the plains. In 1855 he came east to St. Louis, and entered
the St. Louis Medical College — graduating March 1st 1856
before coming to California he went in 1850 to Cleveland O. studied
with Dr. DeLamater and had attended a course of lectures
at the Cleveland Medical College and his course at St. Louis
was the finishing course of his medical education. From
St. Louis he went to Knoxville Ills. where his sister Julia
(wife of Rev. Wm V. Miller) was living. He formed a partnership
with Dr. Reuben Shaw an old practitioner and commenced his
practice as a graduated physician. One of his first cases
was one of surgery, and the patient was one of his young
nephews who in the practicing a "d himself for" a circus
performer, in the very show of his future now. fell and
broke the bridge of his nose. It was a bad break, the
nose was for a time costing over. They have since
in Knoxville a man who a broken nose that on that
account was noted for an entire want of facial beauty.
He was a very worthy man. Smith by name and
was sometimes called "the Smith with the broken
nose" with his face covered with blood. with one hand
to his face trying to find something left of his nose
this wounded nephew ran to his mother at the house
crying "Oh I am ruined I shall live disfigured

(Erastus name was "Marinus — "Rine" for short") ___ under Dr. Phillips ___ soon knew ___ his ___ case of instruments ___ nose, ___ ___ ___ properly ___ so that at this time thought not ___ up to the ___ bridge Phillips stands ___ in ___ &c ___ "Col" ___ like "Marine Smith".

Dr. Phillips married ___ of ___ part of John G. Sanborn ___ ___ ___ 6. 1857. On account of ill health he went to Colorado in 1859, but returned much unimproved in the Spring of 1860, when he went on a farm that he owned near Council Bluffs Ia. He improved a portion of this ___ and continued farming until August 1862, when he returned to ___ and entered the ___ as Ass't. ___ Surgeon of ___ ___ ___. He served ___ in ___ ___ ___ in ___ ___ and Louisiana. ___ the ___ of 1863, when his regiment was stationed at ___ ___ ___ to ___ of ___ he resigned his commission and came ___ . He ___ at ___ Ills and resumed his medical practice, which he still continues at that place. He is now the ___ ___ ___ of Col. William Phillips of ___ His children are as follows —

1729740

1. ELIZABETH	Born March 21. 1855.
2. JOHN SANBORN	" July 7. 1861.
3. EDGAR EVERTSON	" Decem 21. 1865.
4. JULIA	" July 10. 1877.

1 ELIZABETH. Born, March 11. 1855 at Knoxville Ills. She is unmarried and resides with her parents at Galesburg Ills.

2 JOHN SANBORN Born, June 4. 1861. Went Council Bluffs Ia. He graduated at Knox College. After his graduation, he went to Boston Mass, and was one of the editors of "The Wheelman" a magazine. He took a course at Harvard College and graduated in 1885. He then went to Germany, studied and graduated at the University of Leipsic. Returning from abroad he went to New York City and with his friend John S. McClure, founded the New York publishing house of S.S. McClure Co, of which he is the Treasurer. He married Emma, daughter of Curtiss C. West of Oneida Ills. She died in New York City _____ 1888, He again married Jennie daughter of _____ Peterson of Boston. Following are their children

RUTH BEAL   Born July 13. 1891. at Duxbury Mass

DOROTHY SANBORN   "   "   6. 1893. " New York City

MARGARET EVERTSON " November 14. 1897. "   "   "   (last

born of the Phillips (in this line) "as far as advised"

3 EDGAR EVERTSON Born. December 11. 1865 at Galesburg Ills. He married Jennie daughter of Johnson Rickerson of _____ following are their children

WALTER   Born   1888.

LAWRENCE   "   1890.

Wishing to know something of his revolutionary ancestry. some investigations at the <u>NEWBERRY LIBRARY</u> Chicago. great deal of interesting material relating to the [?] American ancestor — on his mothers side. — <u>REV. GEORGE P.</u> Watertown Mass. 1630. and concluded to write for his own & for those of his relations whom it might interest, the review [?] lives of all of the descendants — in the direct line — together with incidents in their lives that might be available. He was [?] in this, by his uncle <u>DR. EDGAR L PHILLIPS</u> of Galesburg Ills living child of Col. William Phillips of Phillipsburgh, was the ol Bible" in his keeping. It contains written family record of birth deaths. College graduations. and other interesting family events. line of descent — <u>Rev George of Watertown 1630</u>. — <u>Rev George of 1664</u>. — <u>Major Moses and Colonel William of Phillipsburgh</u> [?] war period — down to the present time — eleven generations — and [?] seven years unbroken descent.

Ore of the cousins writing from Goshen in reply to [?] inquiry regarding some family dates " <u>Good ancestry</u> is <u>not a thing over which to show</u> certainly is something for which to be [?]

In considering the array of good [?] citizens, — business [?], — scholars, — founders

"Wray Phillips", down to the time of her marriage. A DISTINGUISHED PATRIOT was ..... for as a WASHINGTON .... with the founders of the ...... — .... descendants of Rev. George Phillips of Watertown, and Major Thomas Phillips of Phillips burg, have reason for profound thankfulness, and great personal satisfaction.)

FINIS

CHRISTOPHER PHILLIPS
Born in England, about 1560.

GENERATIONS

1

2   **Rev. George Phillips,** Born / Raised aug: 1593.
  1613.   ... 1617.
  ... Mass. Died 1644.

Theophilus
of Watertown, Mass.

Jonathan
Watertown, Mass.

Joseph
of Oxford, Mass.

3   **Rev. Samuel** Born in Eng: 1625
  1650.
  1656.
  Died in Salisbury, Mass.

Jonathan
Watertown, Mass.

Capt. Stephen
of Salem, Mass.

Israel
of Oxford, Mass.

Daniel
of Charlton, Mass.

4   **Samuel**
  ...

Rev. George — Born 1664
  Graduate of Harvard 1686 — 1696
  Pastor Brookhaven L.I. Died 1739.

Henry Usher

Stephen (Hon?)
of ... Mass.

Justin J.
of Watertown, Mass.

5   **Samuel** (Rev.)
  ...
  Phillip Academy.

George

Moses (Hon Hon.
of Sheffield mass.

William Bill (Col.) Born 1710.
  ... 1800.
  ... 1840.

Albert
of Watertown, Mass.

6   **Rev. Samuel**   **William**
  Boston, Mass.

William
of Smith, Mass.

William
Boston, Mass.

John (Hon)
First Mayor of
Boston, Mass.

7   **Samuel** (Judge)
  Phillips Academy

John
Boston, Mass.

William
Chief Geo.
Mass.

John (Hon.)
First Mayor of
Boston, Mass.

Wendell
Salinguer... Doctor
and Phil and Mass.

8   **John** (Judge)
  ...

Jonathan
Geo. ...

Edward
Boston, Mass.

Edward B.
Boston, Mass. Biography etc.
well (100 vol by...) to
Harvard College.

9   **E. Amiel**
  Watertown, Mass.

A. Buckley

Agnes H. Born 1813.
Mary E.   " 1876.

Frances S. Born 1874.
Northildane " 1876.

(married)
Louis P. Born ...
Henry P. " ...

(married)
Susan E. Born 1841.
Wesley H. " 1843.
William J. " 1845.
Julia P. " 1853.

Rev. Phillips Brooks D.D.

CHRISTOPHER PHILLIPS, ESQ.

HENRY WISNER. DIED 1720. DIED 1790.
Member of 1st 2nd & 3rd Continental Congress 1774—1776.
Signer of the Declaration of Independence.

MAJOR MOSES PHILLIPS. BORN 1741 DIED 1811
Served in Revolutionary War. Maj. 3rd Ulster Co. Reg.
Married Sarah Daughter of HENRY WISNER.

COL. WILLIAM PHILLIPS B. 1772 D 1846
Served in War of 1812 and in Reg. Militia

JOHN E.	SAMUEL B SAMUEL	JULIA	SARAH E	HENRY L.	ELIZABETH P	WILLIAM R	THOMAS S	NICHOLAS E	FREDERICK

JOHN E.
B. Nov 20, 1835
m Elizabeth Wisner
D Dec 7, 1841

SAMUEL B
B
D Oct 22, 1847

SAMUEL
B Sept 22, 1841 Oct 5, 1843
D

JULIA
B June 21, 1811
m Rev Wm. Wilde
Feb 7, 1847

SARAH E
B Apr 30, 1815
D Apr 24, 1846

HENRY L.
Apr. 13, 1813
m Mary Rinenhouse
D May 12, 1814

ELIZABETH P
March 30, 1817
Dr. Henry Hornbeck
March 11, 1845

WILLIAM R
June 9, 1850
Anna M. Edsons
Feb 9, 1845

THOMAS S
Sept 14, 1823
Martha E Zane
April 30, 1876

NICHOLAS E
January 19, 1819
Eliza Adams
June 13, 1896

FREDERICK
April 8, 1771
Mary Gardiner

HENRY AYRES
B Oct 27, 1924
D Sept 23, 1886

ELIZABETH
m Thomas Straight
JOHN STRAIGHT

SARAH WISNER
D Sept 21, 1835
ANNA EVERTSON
B April 1, 1836
m John H. Connor
HARRIET HORNBECK
B July 4, 1840

SARAH EVERTSON
B March 2, 1841
m HENRY HORNBECK
B Victoria 4, 1842
m Dinsmore Rhidy
WILLIAM YOUNG
B October 9, 1845
m Mary Hornly
JULIA PHILLIPS
B August 27, 1871
m A.Th.D. Gumaer

SARAH E
WILLIAM E
HARRIET
WILLIAM E
MARGARET
FREDERICK H.
JULIA

AGNES HAYES
FRANCES JOHNSTON
PHILLIP
KATHERINE

WILLIAM P
FREDERICK
JANE E
EDWIN
FREDERICK

HARRIET COLE
BERTHA

HENRY AYRES
LEWIS EVERTSON
DOROTHY STRAIGHT

EDGAR EVERTSON
JULIA

WALTER
LAWRENCE

RUTH BEAL
DOROTHY STRAIGHT

LOUIS ALISTER
HENRY PHILLIPS

HENRY H. MILLER CHICAGO MAR. 20, 1847.

In Convention of the Representatives of the State of
New York.—Thursday Morning February the 11th 1778.

Col. Van Cortlandt Vice President.

Present for New York. &c. &c.

[list of names, largely illegible]
Col. Lott. &c. &c. ... Morris.
Col. Brewer. Mr. Taylor. ... D. A. Prou...
Mr. Roosevelt. Rev. Livingston. ... Livingston ... Graham.
Capt. Scott. Mr. Schaefer. ... Mr. Miles.
Mr. Harper. ... Mr. ...
... Mr. Webster.
Cumberland Mr. Wisner ... Mr. Harper.
Mr. Stephens

Mr. Wisner Senr, One of the Members, represented to Convention, that he
stands indebted to Oliver DeLancey, now commanding a Brigade in the
actual service of the Enemy, and to David Johnston Esqr. in the Sum
of £ 1760. principal money, for which there is an arrear of interest which
money is secured to be paid by his bond or bonds jointly & a Mortgage
on certain Lands in the County of Ulster. That he is ready to discharge
the said debt, and requests the Direction of this House concerning the
Moiety there' accruing to the said Oliver DeLancey.

Resolved therefore that Mr. Wisner be at liberty to pay one
Moiety of the said debt to Mr. Johnston; and that he ...
other half in the Treasury of this State, to attend to the future
Disposition of the Convention or future Legislature thereof.

that upon producing Mr Johnstons Receipt of Treasurers Certificate
& lodging the same with the Secretary of this Convention, the said
Mortgage shall be null & void, Provided the signing of the said Deed
be at least one witness, or Oath to be administred or due Proof
of, in the Presence thereof by the Chairman of the Committee of S

A Copy   John McKesson Secy to Ct
                                                of the State

Received ye 13 of February 1777 — from Henry Wisner Esqr Seventy
pounds fourteen Shillings and three pence, in the paper Currency
United States and the State of New York, in full of my own
Bond and Mortgage, now in the hands of Oliver DeLancey

£.70:14:3   David Jones

Witnesses present   John Bradner

Personally appeared before me Pierre Van Courtlandt, Vice President of the State of New York, John Bradner of Dutchess Co.
Sworn on the Holy Evangelists of Almighty God dispositor & saith
as a witness the receipt on the other side, and said David
the same as his voluntary Act and Deed for the uses th
Sworn this 25th of April 1777 in Kingston before me
                              Pierre Van Courtlandt

True Copies of a Receipt and the proof thereof filed
of the Convention

                    John McKesson &c

4

I do acknowledge that Henry Wisner Esqr. was paid into the Treasury of the State of New York, Seven hundred and twenty three Pounds, twelve Shillings, and three pence, pursuant to a Resolution of the Convention of this State of the 11th of February last, being the principal & Interest, since to be due from him, on a Bond and Mortgage to Oliver DeLancey Esqr. and David Johnston Esqr. for P. V. B. Livingston Esqr. Treasurer.

           Gerard Bancker

Witness

    John McKesson

    Secy. to the Convention of the State of New York

5030

www.ingramcontent.com/pod-product-compliance
Lightning Source LLC
Chambersburg PA
CBHW022150090426
42742CB00010B/1452